HOW TO

SET A TABLE

—

CLARKSON POTTER/PUBLISHERS NEW YORK

CONTENTS

*"One cannot think well, love well,
sleep well, if one has not dined well."*

———

VIRGINIA WOOLF

INTRODUCTION

Whether you're throwing a dinner party for twelve or sharing takeout for two, a thoughtful setting can make any meal feel special. Formal or casual, traditional or modern, colorful or neutral, patterned or plain, your table should reflect your style.

Trying to keep track of all the rules can seem intimidating. But with a few simple guidelines, almost anything goes: mix and match, repurpose pieces, and incorporate vintage finds. Think about dressing a table as if you were putting together a great outfit—personality is always the most important ingredient.

This handbook will help you navigate the nuances of table settings, fill your cupboards with pieces you love, and find new ways to use them in any space. As your tastes evolve, so will your collection—have fun with it!

PICKING YOUR PIECES

Dinnerware Basics

Whichever dishes you decide on, dinnerware is meant to be used. Think about what kinds of food you like to eat and how you tend to entertain, then pick the pieces that make sense. A good number to start with is eight settings, or twelve if you have people over often.

CHOOSE YOUR TYPE

PORCELAIN

A slightly translucent ceramic made by firing quality clays at extremely high temperatures, porcelain is generally very durable, resistant to stains, and dishwasher-, oven-, and microwave-safe (with the exception of metallic or highly decorated pieces) despite its delicate appearance.

EARTHENWARE

Made from less refined clays and fired at lower temperatures, earthenware is porous and less resistant to chipping. Glazes are often added to make pieces more durable and nonabsorbent.

STONEWARE

Combining porcelain's resilience with the casual look of earthenware, these chip-resistant and nonporous pieces are made by firing dense clay at high temperatures.

Table **TALK**

BECAUSE THE CHINESE FIRST CAME UP WITH THE FORMULA TO MAKE PORCELAIN, "CHINA" IS OFTEN USED AS A GENERAL TERM FOR FINE PORCELAIN.

SELECT YOUR SET

Many companies offer dinnerware in four- or five-piece sets. The most common include a dinner plate, a salad plate, a bowl, and a mug. A slightly more formal option substitutes the bowl for a bread-and-butter plate and the mug for a cup and saucer.

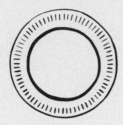

DINNER PLATE
At 10 to 11 inches in diameter, the most common styles are the coupe and traditional rim.

SALAD PLATE
From 7½ to 8½ inches in diameter, this is easily adaptable for dessert, lunch, or tea.

BOWLS
Rim or coupe, shallow or deep, bowls are traditionally used for soup, pasta, and cereal. Fruit bowls are slightly smaller and are perfect for desserts and vegetable sides.

CUPS & SAUCERS
A standard coffee cup holds 6 to 8 ounces. A large breakfast cup or mug is made for 11 to 12 ounces.

ADD À LA CARTE

It's also common to purchase open stock pieces. You can pick each dish individually or add to existing sets. Below are some additional styles to consider:

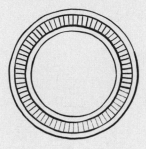

CHARGER

Generally 11 to 14 inches in diameter, this large piece isn't meant to hold food. Instead, it serves as a placeholder for the dinner plate and can be left on the table as a base for the salad plate or soup bowl.

BREAD & BUTTER PLATE

Between 6 and 6½ inches, it's also perfectly sized for breakfast or to use under desserts served in stemmed glasses.

DESSERT PLATE

Slightly smaller than a salad plate, the two can be used interchangeably.

A flexible and economical approach is to pick just a dinner plate and a shallow bowl, which can be used for soup, salad, cereal, and dessert.

CHOOSE YOUR SERVING PIECES

As long as you have a mix of shapes and sizes, these pieces can serve multiple purposes, and they're fun to collect over time.

SOUP TUREEN
Highly decorative yet functional, this is one of the largest serving pieces and includes a cover to keep food warm.

GRAVY BOAT
For gravy as well as dressings and other sauces, it should be accompanied by a ladle to help avoid a mess.

PLATTERS
Whether oval or round, covered or open, these are good for vegetables, grains, and meats.

BOWLS
Large, deep bowls are perfect for salads and sides.

If space is an issue, nesting bowls that stack inside one another are a smart choice.

Glasses at a Glance

Designed with specific drinks in mind, certain shapes can enhance flavors and ingredients, but feel free to mix them up.

TUMBLER
Usually made to hold 8 ounces, it's used for water, juice, or soda.

WINEGLASSES
Red wine is best in larger styles with wide bowls to encourage oxidation. White is served in styles with narrower tops.

CHAMPAGNE GLASSES
A tall, narrow flute helps keep fizz from going flat. A shallow, saucer-shaped coupe strikes a vintage speakeasy vibe.

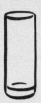

HIGHBALL
This taller glass is used mainly for mixed drinks.

OLD-FASHIONED
Also called a lowball or rocks glass, it has a thick base that allows ingredients to be muddled.

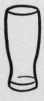

PILSNER
Tall with a slight taper, it's made to showcase lighter pale ales but can be used for any beer.

BRANDY SNIFTER
Great for after-dinner drinks, a wide-bottomed bowl that gets narrower at the top helps capture the alcohol's aromas.

Flatware Essentials

While dozens of specialty pieces were once common, like the asparagus fork and the fruit spoon, today a standard set generally includes five pieces—a dinner knife, two forks (one for dinner, the other for salad or dessert), and two spoons (one slightly larger for soup, the other slightly smaller for tea or coffee).

As with dinnerware, eight to twelve sets is a good place to start. Sterling silver can be expensive but it will last forever. Whichever material or style you choose, look for pieces that have a little bit of weight and a nice feel in the hand.

Always shine silver with good-quality polish, rinse well, and dry thoroughly with a soft linen cloth to avoid spotting. Be careful not to polish roughly or too often—too much buffing can take off the top layer, including any monograms.

STERLING SILVER

Recognized by its stamp, sterling silver is mixed with a small amount of hard alloy metal for strength at a ratio of 92.5 percent pure silver to 7.5 percent copper.

SILVER PLATE

Less expensive but with the same warmth as sterling, these pieces are made from a base metal like nickel or copper that is plated with silver.

STAINLESS STEEL

Low maintenance and usually the most common choice, stainless is made from an alloy of iron, chromium, and nickel.

Salad
FORK

Dinner
FORK

Dinner
KNIFE

Soup
SPOON

Coffee
SPOON

The Linen Drawer

One of the easiest ways to add texture, color, and pattern, table linens can transform the look and mood of a meal. If you have trouble choosing, you can never go wrong with softer colors and timeless patterns that you won't tire of too quickly.

Table linens should be washable, and cotton tends to be the easiest to care for. Linen is lovely, but it wrinkles easily and requires extra ironing if you want to keep it crisp. Damask is one of the most formal and traditional choices—made with silk, linen, and other natural fibers, it has a reversible pattern woven into it.

For a perfectly pressed tablecloth: dampen the fabric with warm water, lay it over a terry-cloth towel, and use a steam iron.

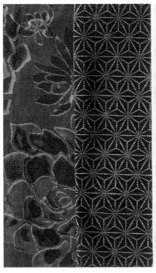
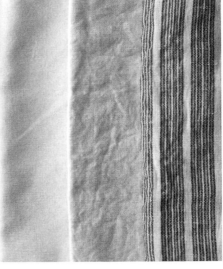

TABLECLOTHS

As a general rule, these should fall 12 to 15 inches from the edge of the table.

NAPKINS

Fold them, roll them, tuck them in to glasses, or hold them together with rings—the presentation possibilities are endless.

Common Sizes

DINNER
22 to 26 inches square

LUNCHEON
14 to 18 inches square

COCKTAIL
4 to 6 inches square

RUNNERS

One of the most flexible options, they fit on any size table or buffet.

PLACE MATS

More casual than a tablecloth, these protect the table and visually divide the surface into "places."

A NOTE ON MONOGRAMS

A single letter (traditionally the first letter of the last name) is simple and elegant. The most common placement is either on the lower right-hand corner or directly in the center of the napkins.

PUTTING IT ALL
TOGETHER

The Casual Setting

An informal setting has only a few pieces, and everything that's needed throughout the meal should be laid out at once. It's good for family-style spreads and dinners that don't require resetting during service. As a general rule for any occasion (casual or formal), plates and flatware should be placed about ½ inch apart, with the bottoms lined up about an inch from the edge of the table, and each person should be given about 24 inches of table space to avoid feeling squished.

1 | **DINNER PLATE**

2 | **NAPKIN**

3 | **DINNER FORK**

4 | **DINNER KNIFE**

5 | **SOUP SPOON**

6 | **WATER GLASS**

7 | **WINEGLASS**

Napkin rings are a quick way to keep linens neat and pulled together.

The Formal Setting

A formal table setting requires a more hands-on approach to service. Oftentimes, there are many pieces on the table to start, and plates and flatware need to be cleared between courses. Settings for no more than three courses should be laid out at a time—and forks, knives, and spoons are always placed in order of use, from the outside in.

1 | **DINNER PLATE**

2 | **SALAD PLATE**

3 | **BREAD-AND-BUTTER PLATE**

4 | **BREAD KNIFE**

5 | **SALAD FORK**

6 | **DINNER FORK**

7 | **DINNER KNIFE**

8 | **SOUP SPOON**

9 | **DESSERT SPOON**

10 | **WHITE WINE GLASS**

11 | **WATER GLASS**

12 | **RED WINE GLASS**

13 | **NAPKIN**

14 | **PLACE CARD**

Plates are served to the left of guests and cleared from the right.
All plates, serving dishes, and condiments should be removed from
the table before dessert is served.

Mixing & Matching

This is where table setting gets playful. Generally, white dinner plates are the most versatile and put the spotlight on the food. Dessert plates are a good place to experiment with pattern—a piece of chocolate cake will look good on just about anything. White or neutral serving pieces lighten up the table. Colorful ones make more of a statement.

USING COLOR

When picking palettes, consider the colors in the room where you eat. Complementary colors (ones on opposite sides of the color wheel) always work well together, and don't forget to think about scale—balance intricate designs and saturated solids with something more neutral.

COLLECTING ANTIQUES

Treasures can be found at estate sales, thrift shops, and in your grandma's attic. Look for serving pieces, silverware, cut or colored glass, and pretty plates and platters. Always check antique pieces carefully (both tops and bottoms) before you buy, watching out for chips, hairlines, and cracks.

If you're buying a dessert and a salad set, choose different patterns so you have more options (they're almost the same size and can be used interchangeably).

If you stick with a cohesive palette, it's easier to mix patterns. Pick solid plates that pull from a color in something printed.

INCORPORATING HEIRLOOMS

For an eclectic look, mix antique silver together. Or pair vintage dessert plates with newer dinnerware.

TONAL TEXTURE

All-white doesn't have to be boring. Patterns in relief and simple borders add depth and dimension.

Napkin Folding

There are endless ways to present napkins at the table, from intricate designs to casual folds. We've included a couple of our favorites here.

It's polite to place your napkin on your chair if you need to get up during a meal.

THE DIAMOND FOLD

1 | Lay the napkin face down in front of you. Fold it in half from top to bottom, and then again from left to right. You should have a smaller square with the open end facing toward you.

2 | Fold back the top layer so that its bottom right corner touches the upper left-hand corner of the napkin.

3 | Fold back the second layer just as you did the first, but stop slightly short of the last fold to create an even, staggered effect. Repeat until you have folded back all of the remaining layers.

4 | Rotate the napkin clockwise until the point of the triangle shape is at the top. Flip the napkin over. Fold both bottom corners toward the top center point, overlapping them a little so that you end up with a five-sided diamond shape. Carefully turn the napkin over and flatten or iron it. Place the napkin on the plate.

If you have herbs left over from cooking, use them to decorate the table.

THE SINGLE POCKET FOLD

1 | Lay the napkin facedown in front of you. Fold the napkin in half from the bottom to the top to form a rectangle with the open end facing away from you.

2 | Fold the top layer halfway back. Flip the napkin over.

3 | Fold the napkin in half from the right to the left, and then in half again from right to left.

4 | Carefully flip the napkin over. Tie a bit of twine into a bow around the bottom half of the napkin. Tuck in a sprig of rosemary or another herb or flower as an embellishment. Insert a menu card and place the napkin on the plate.

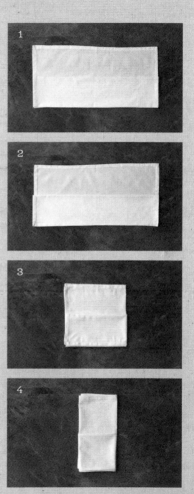

Finishing Touches

Whatever decorations you choose,
remember that they shouldn't distract
from the food or conversation.

CANDLES
Lots of little votives can have a magical
effect. A single candelabra is classic.

A tip for picking flowers: choose something that's in season and complements a color from your dishes or linens.

FLOWERS & GARLANDS

Keep arrangements low enough that they don't block guests from talking across the table. If you have a large centerpiece, remove it just before the guests take their seats.

NATURAL INGREDIENTS

Anything pretty and fresh that's used to make a meal can also be used to garnish a place setting.

The
DINING TABLE

SUNDAY SUPPER

It's nice to end the week with a casual, family-style meal—usually eaten in the late afternoon. Set a simple table with large plates, basic linens, and serving dishes ready so guests can help themselves.

Leftovers are perfect for weekday lunches—as sandwich meat, in scrambles, or for savory pie fillings. Set out containers ahead of dinner, so they're easy to fill when everyone is finished.

Table TALK

SUNDAY ROASTS ORIGINATED IN ENGLAND. TRADITIONALLY, MANY ANGLICANS AND CATHOLICS DIDN'T EAT MEAT FROM FRIDAY NIGHT THROUGH CHURCH ON SUNDAY. THE ROAST WAS A CELEBRATORY MEAL EATEN AFTER THE SERVICE WHEN THE FAST WAS FINALLY BROKEN.

THE FOUNDATION
OF A FAMILY-STYLE FEAST

PLATTERS FOR SERVING
A roasting dish that can go straight from the oven
to the table means fewer dishes to do later.

BOWLS TO PASS
Keep serving utensils in serving bowls so it's easy for
guests to help themselves, and always pass to the right.

SMALL DISHES FOR BUTTER,
SALT, AND PEPPER
Salt and pepper should travel as a pair. Make sure
to try the food before adding extra seasoning.

SEATED DINNER PARTY

For special occasions or just because, a meal served in courses doesn't need to be complicated. A palette of white and gold is clean and classic—and allows the food to take center stage.

Traditionally, the dinner plate is brought out after the first course and charger are cleared—for something simpler, layer the dinner plate with a salad plate, which can be removed after the appetizer.

THE BASICS FOR A FORMAL (NOT FUSSY) AFFAIR

PLACE CARDS

Use them for parties of eight or more. A menu card is a nice way to guide guests through multiple courses.

The host or hostess generally sits at the head of the table where he or she can see and engage all of the guests.

GLASSES

Set the water glass to the right of the plate just above the knife. Wineglasses are set to the right of the water glass, in the order that they will be used.

FLATWARE

Once used, silver shouldn't touch the table. Rest it on the edge of a plate or saucer instead.

FOLDED NAPKINS

Place on your lap right after sitting.

ALWAYS WAIT UNTIL EVERYONE IS SERVED BEFORE YOU START EATING, AND DON'T CLEAR PLATES BEFORE THE LAST GUEST IS FINISHED.

HOLIDAY BREAKFAST

On long weekends, you might want to serve a more elaborate morning meal. Start with plates, a small bowl, and a napkin at each place, and fill the table with fresh flowers that celebrate the season.

For make-your-own brunch cocktails, set up a simple bar on a side table with juices, Bloody Mary mix, vodka, and champagne.

ESSENTIALS FOR
CHRISTMAS MORNING

FRENCH PRESS COFFEE MAKER
Keep things easy and use the same piece for
brewing and serving at the table.

MULTIPURPOSE TUMBLERS
A simple glass works for water, juice,
mimosas, or milk.

SERVING DISHES
Prepare food on cutting boards and in ceramics that
can go straight from the kitchen to the table.

CLEAR BOTTLES & GLASSES
Decant condiments such as maple syrup
for a cleaner spread.

The
BREAKFAST BAR

APPETIZERS & COCKTAILS

If you don't have a lot of space, spread out antipasto and other small bites on a breakfast bar or butcher block. Stack salad or bread-and-butter plates so people can help themselves.

A mix of mismatched plates make it easy for guests to remember whose is whose if they rest them on a side or coffee table.

THE ELEMENTS OF
A SIMPLE SPEAKEASY

TRAY AS A BAR
A bar cart isn't necessary—just use a tray to
corral liquor, shakers, and stir sticks.

———————————

A few classic mixers to always have on hand:
Rose's Lime Juice, ginger beer, tonic water (in small bottles,
so it doesn't go flat), club soda, bitters.

A MIX OF COCKTAIL GLASSES
Don't worry if you don't have complete sets—
put out a selection and let guests choose the
style they like best.

MISMATCHED SILVER & TONGS
Use a mix of vintage and new silver for hors d'oeuvres.

WEEKEND BREAKFAST

Especially good when you have company, a help-yourself spread is ready whether guests get up early or sleep late.

Lay out stacks of plates, bowls, and mugs the night before, along with cereal, sugar, and jams.

Keep a basket with milk, cream, and butter in the fridge—and leave a notecard explaining where to find things.

WAYS TO MAKE OVERNIGHT
GUESTS FEEL AT HOME

COFFEE MAKER & MUGS
A pour-over pot with filters is great for
individual cups.

EGG CUPS FOR SERVING
Hardboil eggs the night before and leave them
out in pretty cups.

A CONTAINER FOR FLATWARE
Use a mason jar, wide-mouthed glass, or mug to keep
knives, forks, and spoons neatly together.

Table
TALK

MAKE SURE A COVERED JAR OF
FRESHLY GROUND BEANS IS NEARBY.

MIDNIGHT BITES

Late at night is the perfect time for leftovers and a cold drink—the adult version of a bedtime snack. Instead of standing over the sink or eating directly from the take-out box, set up a small spread on the breakfast bar. Put pizza on plates, pour beer into glasses, and use real linens.

Fresh dish towels from the kitchen make great stand-ins for place mats and napkins.

NIGHTTIME SNACK SUPPLIES

PINCH BOWLS FOR SEASONING
Fill with salt, Parmesan, or chili flakes.

GLASSES FOR WINE OR BEER
Pour bottled beer into tumblers or stemmed goblets.

SMALL PLATES
Use anything except paper—even fine china.

---

*Soak dishes in the sink before going to bed so
cleanup is faster in the morning.*

The
COFFEE TABLE

TUESDAY TAKEOUT

Easy-to-eat noodle and rice dishes are perfect for perching on a coffee table. It's nice to replate entrées and to decant sauces before serving.

Coasters are an easy way to add pattern. Use them under glasses and small dishes of sauces.

THE DETAILS IN
DECANTING DELIVERY

A RUNNER FOR SMALLER TABLES
Long and narrow, it fits on almost any surface.
As an alternative, use tea towels or unfolded
napkins as place mats.

DINNERWARE AS SERVING DISHES
Dinner plates and cereal bowls are just the right
size for smaller portions.

CHOPSTICKS
Rest them on the edge of your plate when
you're not using them.

Table
TALK

HOLD THE UPPER CHOPSTICK LIKE A PENCIL,
BETWEEN YOUR THUMB AND INDEX FINGER, JUST
ABOVE THE MIDDLE. THE SECOND CHOPSTICK
SHOULD BE PARALLEL, HELD AGAINST YOUR RING
FINGER AND THE BASE OF YOUR THUMB.

MOVIE NIGHT

Elevate a night of Netflix or celebrate the Oscars with snacks served in Art Deco–style porcelain, and drinks in fancy glasses.

Mix metallics and votive candles for a warm glow and a hit of shine.

AN OSCAR NIGHT
ARRANGEMENT

NAPKINS & RINGS

Think of napkin rings as jewelry for the table.
Play with different shapes and materials as you
would a stack of bangles or cocktail rings.

A SOUP TUREEN FOR POPCORN

Repurpose a vintage piece for serving snacks.

A MIX OF PATTERNED PLATES & BOWLS

The Academy Awards are the perfect time to flaunt
your best porcelain—even if it doesn't match.

———————

*Decorative dessert plates can be expensive and might
seem extravagant to purchase as a set. Instead, just buy
a few and use them as accents.*

WINE &
CHEESE

Served before dinner, after
dinner, or as a meal on its own,
wine and cheese is the perfect
spread for a coffee table,
where food can be nibbled and
nothing needs to be cut.

---

*To build a cheese board, choose at least
three varieties and include a mix of
milks, flavors, and textures—plus a knife
for each.*

THE PERFECT ASSORTMENT

CHEESE BOARD
Slate is a nice alternative to wood, and you can
use chalk to write the names of the cheese.

A BOWL USED AS AN ICE BUCKET
Almost any large serving bowl will work—choose
something patterned for a pop of color.

_____

*Chill white wine ahead of time and open a few bottles before
guests arrive. Some white wines aren't meant to be ice cold—
check with your local wine store for the ideal temperature.*

A MIX OF GLASSES
Mix stemmed styles with tumblers for a casual
vibe (or if you don't have a complete set).

SMALL BOWLS AND SPOONS
Use these for plating nuts, olives, crackers, and
chutney. Don't forget one for olive pits.

The
PICNIC BLANKET

BIRTHDAY
PICNIC

Gather things together in a
basket, including a fancy cake
stand and champagne coupes.
Then head to the park
or patio.

*Make transporting everything easier
by asking each guest to contribute—
have someone bring the cake and
candles, someone else can take care
of the champagne and glasses,
and so on.*

FESTIVE TOUCHES

PICNIC BASKET
Fill it with china and glasses instead of paper
picnicware. Wrap fabric napkins around the champagne
coupes to pad them while carrying them to the park.

THE CHAMPAGNE COUPE HAS A VINTAGE VIBE.
IT WAS INTRODUCED IN FRANCE DURING THE
EIGHTEENTH CENTURY AND BECAME FASHIONABLE
IN THE UNITED STATES IN THE 1930S.

LINENS & BLANKETS
Use real tablecloths and napkins—just layer them
over a heavier picnic blanket to avoid grass stains.

CAKE STAND
Top with a cake—or put candles on stacks of cupcakes,
muffins, or sandwiches to make them feel festive.

BACKYARD BBQ

A summer cookout should feel relaxed—keep the menu simple and serve food family-style so guests can help themselves.

A good playlist keeps the momentum going throughout the meal without distracting from conversation—nothing too loud or too slow. Think about how long the party will last and make sure there are enough songs to fill the time.

COOKOUT BASICS

PLATES
Repurpose extra dinner plates as trays for toppings
and sides. Use smaller sizes for spoon rests.

JAM JARS FOR CONDIMENTS
Fill covered containers to transport ketchup, mustard,
and relishes in just the right portions.

WOODEN TRAYS FOR BREAD
Something long and narrow is great for laying
out hamburger buns.

BBQ TOOLS
Use the same utensils to cook and to serve:
tongs, spatulas, and spoons.

The
BISTRO TABLE

WEEKDAY BREAKFAST

Even on a busy morning when there's no time to cook, it's nice to sit down for breakfast. A plate, spoon, and coffee cup are all you really need, but adding egg cups, juice glasses, and linens makes it feel luxurious.

Set out dishes the night before so everything's ready to go when you wake up.

THE MORNING MIX

BOWLS
One of the most versatile dishes, they can be
used to serve almost anything.

————————

*For a Parisian twist, drink coffee out of small
bowls instead of mugs.*

TABLE LINENS
A runner fits on any table, regardless of size.

————————

*To keep cloth napkins, runners, and place mats smooth,
store them wrapped around a paper tube.*

CUPS FOR EGGS
If you don't have traditional egg cups, espresso
cups are a similar size and will work just as well.

DINNER
FOR TWO

Don't save fine china just
for special occasions. Use
it for dinner any day of the
week. A simple two-course
meal feels intimate served
on a small bistro table. It can
be charming to mix sets of
plates and play with different
patterns.

---

*Make it feel like a local restaurant: use
a white tablecloth, light a single votive
candle, and fill a small bud vase with
fresh flowers.*

DATE-NIGHT INSPIRATION

VOTIVE HOLDERS FOR CANDLES
AND FLOWERS
An easy way to set the mood and create
the most flattering light.

PRETTY PLATES
Layer different styles—interesting edges stand
out against a pattern and color.

A BASKET OR BOWL FOR BREAD
Line it with a linen napkin to keep rolls
covered and warm.

A PLATE FOR BUTTER
Pick a small saucer or salad plate if you don't
have a designated dish.

Table
TALK

USE A BUTTER KNIFE TO PUT A PORTION
ONTO YOUR PLATE—NEVER SPREAD
DIRECTLY ONTO THE BREAD.

The
CONSOLE

DESSERT &
CHAMPAGNE

A sideboard or console
works as a serving station for
after-dinner treats. Set out
platters of cakes and cookies,
and stacks of small plates
and napkins.

---

*For an easy cocktail that guests can
make themselves, provide a simple
herbal or fruit syrup to mix with
champagne. Also include sparkling
water or soda for an option
without alcohol.*

IDEAS FOR A SPARKLING CELEBRATION

TIERED STANDS

If you have any special serving pieces, use them
to add height—a decorative cake stand makes
even a simple dessert look fancy.

ICE BUCKET

Keep this at the edge of the table so guests can easily
refill their glasses without waiting in the dessert line.

---

*To chill champagne quickly, put the bottle in a mix
of water and ice.*

TRAYS AND BOARDS

Mix materials—marble, brass, wood, or lacquer—
to add texture and color.

OPEN HOUSE

If hosting a dinner party with lots of guests seems scary, an open house is an easy way to entertain. Hours are usually open-ended, so you don't need to scramble to get everything on the table at a certain time. People will come and go, creating a casual, laid-back vibe.

Open houses are common around the holidays, but you can throw one any time. Plan something around a graduation, a new move, or a big game.

TIPS FOR EASY ENTERTAINING

SERVING BOWLS

Set each dish out next to any seasoning or condiments that might be needed. Place a cutting board nearby for resting serving spoons.

Texture and height are important on buffets. Berry boxes from the farmer's market make great risers, napkin holders, or bread boxes.

A PUNCH BOWL

Batch drinks ahead of time and let guests ladle their own.

FLATWARE

Bundle sets up in napkins and tie with simple twine so they're easy to grab.

POTLUCK
DINNER

Serve dinner from a buffet if
you don't have a big table, and
have each guest bring a dish
to pass. It's important to lay
things out in the order that
people will serve themselves—
with plates at the beginning
and utensils at the end.

---

*Party ideas: pick a theme or cuisine for
the night. Or start a cooking club to
exchange recipes where everyone takes
turn hosting.*

CROWD-PLEASING PIECES

SERVING BOWLS & PLATTERS

Keep dressings next to salads and seasonings
near main courses.

---

*If possible, leave a little bit of space between each
dish so people can put down their plates and use
both hands for serving.*

CHARGERS AS DINNER PLATES

The larger size lends itself to bigger portions.

FLATWARE ROLLED IN NAPKINS

These should be stacked at the end of the buffet for
guests to grab after they've filled their plates.

The
SERVING TRAY

BREAKFAST
IN BED

This is a sweet surprise for special days. Pick a tray that's just large enough to hold everything comfortably and that's easy to carry from the kitchen to the bedroom.

Keep the menu simple: Focus on things you can prepare ahead of time, hot foods that cook fast, like scrambled eggs, ready-made pastries or bagels, and things that are good at room temperature, like fruit, yogurt, and granola.

LAZY MORNING MUST-HAVES

STURDY DISHES
Choose bowls and mugs with wide bottoms for stability,
and plates that are large enough to catch crumbs.

A CARAFE OR SMALL PITCHER FOR REFILLS
Include extra coffee, juice, or water so you don't
need to run back to the kitchen for a top-off.

_____

Avoid using stemmed glasses or anything top heavy
that might tip over.

A GLASS FOR FLOWERS
Keep decorations minimal. A single flower
or petite bouquet in a bottle, water glass, or bud vase
is perfect for small spaces.

AFTERNOON TEA

Traditionally served around three or four, tea and treats are a child-friendly alternative to cocktail hour. Use a tray to corral and carry a teapot, cups, milk, and sugar to the living or dining room.

Table
TALK

AFTERNOON TEA BECAME POPULAR IN NINETEENTH-CENTURY ENGLAND. AS LEGEND GOES, IT STARTED WHEN ANNA MARIA RUSSELL, DUCHESS OF BEDFORD, NEEDED A PICK-ME-UP BETWEEN LUNCH AND A LATE DINNER. HER FRIENDS STARTED JOINING HER AND SOON IT BECAME A SOCIAL AFFAIR.

TEATIME NECESSITIES

TEAPOT
It doesn't need to be from the same collection
as the cups and saucers. Mix in vintage pieces
or family heirlooms.

---

*Include a pitcher or pot of hot water for those
who like to dilute their tea.*

TEACUPS & SAUCERS
Make sure each guest has his or her own teaspoon
for stirring in cream and sugar.

DESSERT OR SALAD PLATES
Stack them and layer each with a cocktail
napkin to save space.

A SUGAR BOWL, CREAMER & SAUCER
FOR LEMON SLICES
Pair loose sugar with a spoon, cubes with tongs,
and citrus with a small fork.

Resources

ABC CARPET & HOME
abchome.com

AMAZON
amazon.com

ANTHROPOLOGIE*
anthropologie.com

APARTMENT THERAPY FOR CANVAS*
apartmenttherapy.com

BARDITH
bardith.com

BED BATH & BEYOND
bedbathandbeyond.com

BERNARDAUD
bernardaud.com

BLOOMINGDALE'S
bloomingdales.com

CHILEWICH (PLACE MAT)*
chilewich.com

CLAM LAB (CERAMICS)*
clamlab.com

CRATE & BARREL
crateandbarrel.com

CUTIPOL CUTLERY*
cutipol.pt

FISHS EDDY
fishseddy.com

GLOBAL TABLE
globaltable.com

HEATH CERAMICS
heathceramics.com

JONATHAN ADLER
jonathanadler.com

KATE SPADE*
katespade.com

LENOX*
lenox.com

MACY'S*
macys.com

MICHAEL C. FINA
michaelcfina.com

POTTERY BARN
potterybarn.com

REPLACEMENTS, LTD.
replacements.com

RESTORATION HARDWARE
restorationhardware.com

SCULLY & SCULLY
scullyandscully.com

SNOWE
snowehome.com

SUR LA TABLE
surlatable.com

TARGET*
target.com

URBAN OUTFITTERS*
urbanoutfitters.com

WILLIAMS SONOMA*
williams-sonoma.com

WEST ELM*
westelm.com

A SPECIAL THANK-YOU TO THESE ADVISORS AND CONSULTANTS:

Kristen Usui (kristenusui.com), for her gorgeous flower arrangements, and Shadow at J-Rose Wholesale Flowers, for donating the flowers

Kristin Perrakis, Jean Armstrong, and Michael Schwarz, for lending props from Williams Sonoma

Naomi Nomikos at Bardith

Sophie Raubiet at Bernardaud

Nathalie Smith at Global Table

Jamie Erickson at Poppy's

Copyright © 2017 by Clarkson Potter/Publishers,
an imprint of the Crown Publishing Group,
a division of Penguin Random House LLC

Published in the United States by Clarkson Potter/Publishers,
an imprint of the Crown Publishing Group, a division
of Penguin Random House LLC, New York.

crownpublishing.com
clarksonpotter.com

Library of Congress Cataloging-in-Publication Data
Names: Smoot, Alpha, photographer.
Title: How to set a table / photographs by Alpha Smoot ;
styling by Maeve Sheridan.
Description: First edition. | New York : Clarkson Potter/
Publishers, [2017]
Identifiers: LCCN 2016044389| ISBN 9780451498021
(paperback) | ISBN 9780451498038 (eISBN)
Subjects: LCSH: Table setting and decoration. | Entertaining.
Classification: LCC TX871 .L54 2017 | DDC 642/.6--dc23
LC record available at https://lccn.loc.gov/2016044389

ISBN 978-0-451-49802-1
Ebook ISBN 978-0-451-49803-8

Printed in China

WRITTEN BY Chloe Lieske
INTERIOR PHOTOGRAPHS BY Alpha Smoot
ILLUSTRATIONS BY woolypear
PROP STYLING BY Maeve Sheridan
FLORAL STYLING BY Kristen Usui
COVER AND INTERIOR DESIGN BY Danielle Deschenes

10 9 8 7 6 5 4 3 2 1

First Edition